Alexis Kimbembi Ma Ibaka

Caves with blind fish

Alexis Kimbembi Ma Ibaka

Caves with blind fish

Caecobarbus geertsii de Mbanza-Ngungu en R.D.Congo

ScienciaScripts

Imprint

Any brand names and product names mentioned in this book are subject to trademark, brand or patent protection and are trademarks or registered trademarks of their respective holders. The use of brand names, product names, common names, trade names, product descriptions etc. even without a particular marking in this work is in no way to be construed to mean that such names may be regarded as unrestricted in respect of trademark and brand protection legislation and could thus be used by anyone.

Cover image: www.ingimage.com

This book is a translation from the original published under ISBN 978-620-2-27883-6.

Publisher:
Sciencia Scripts
is a trademark of
Dodo Books Indian Ocean Ltd. and OmniScriptum S.R.L publishing group

120 High Road, East Finchley, London, N2 9ED, United Kingdom
Str. Armeneasca 28/1, office 1, Chisinau MD-2012, Republic of Moldova, Europe
Printed at: see last page
ISBN: 978-620-5-93210-0

Table of contents :

Caves with blind fish, Caecobarbus geertsii of Mbanza-Ngungu in D.R. Congo

Potential world heritage property that deserves conservation, unfortunately in degradation.

2018

**By Alexis
KIMBEMBI**

Acknowledgements

I would like to thank Professor Michel Maldague for having accepted to review this study.

My special gratitude to my parent institution, the Institut Supérieur Pédagogique de Mbanza-Ngungu for opening my mind to these kinds of research.

I would like to thank Editions Universitaires Européennes for having encouraged me to publish my first data on the state of the caves of *Caecobarbus geertsii in* the Territory of Mbanza-Ngungu in R.D.Congo.

The outcome of this work is inconceivable without multiple collaborations of all kinds, ranging from field work to manuscript reviews. My gratitude goes to Dr. Emmanuel Vreven for having had the concern to come to live the realities of the field, to Professor Soleil Wamuini for his accompaniment, to the local political-administrative authorities for having authorized us to carry out our investigations in their territory and to the population which borders the caves for having facilitated our entry into their mystical environments.

INTRODUCTION

The idea of working on the Mbanza-Ngungu caves dates back to my doctoral training at the Ecole Régionale Post-Universitaire en Aménagement et Gestion Intégrés des Forêts et Territoires tropicaux (ERAIFT), University of Kinshasa, from 1999 to 2007. Indeed, in the Democratic Republic of Congo, in this field of speleology, the first works were respectively related to the geography and ecology of the caves of Bas-Congo (Leleup and Heuts, 1954), to the cave fauna of the Belgian Congo (Leleup, 1956) and to the variation and adaptation of *Caecobarbus geertsii* Blgr (Heuts, 1951).

Today, the galloping demographic growth and the distortion of development in favor of cities in developing countries have resulted in rural exodus. These migrations are the result of the destabilization of rural communities and the degradation of their natural resources. We know the consequences that result from these phenomena. To the extension of the hasty and anarchic urbanization, is added the lack of employment which has a meaning. Faced with this situation, the alternative activity for the survival of the urban population remains agriculture, in all its forms in the areas adjacent to the urban areas.

The town of Mbanza-Ngungu is not immune to this problem. This is evidenced by the clearing of the hills where the caves are located, as a result of slash-and-burn cultivation, associated with the technique of fire-sweeping. These anthropic pressures constitute threats to this area close to the threshold of irreversibility, which is essential for the conservation of *Caecobarbus geertsii* (Kimbembi, 2012). The presence of blind fish caves is an emerging feature of the Central Kongo Province in D.R.Congo.

The present work is the result not only of data from my doctoral dissertation (Kimbembi, 2007) but also of data updated during the process of a decade of continuous monitoring of the cave area in Mbanza-Ngungu Territory.

Our attention was focused on *Caecobarbus geertsii* listed as vulnerable (Lévêque and Daget, 1984). A vulnerable species is a species facing a high risk of extinction in the wild (IUCN, 2001). This species is listed in Appendix II of CITES (MECNPF, 1998). This implies *ipso facto* the protection of its habitat, the caves.

However, such a listing should in principle promote the taking of concrete protection and development measures aimed at conserving and increasing these renewable natural resources, threatened with extinction. This is not the case for this endemic species that depends on the caves of Mbanza-Ngungu.

Indeed, two out of eight caves with *Caecobarbus geertsii* inventoried by Heuts and Leleup (1954) have disappeared (B 20 and B 21). The condition of two other caves (Gas Cave and Cascades Cave) out of the six remaining is unknown. Of the four remaining former caves (Lukatu, Kiamwu, Nkiengie, and Nenga), Nenga Cave has not yet been found. Of these three former remaining localities, since 2017, more specimens of this fish are observed in the Lukatu cave. This means that only two former caves remain.

In addition to these two old caves, ten other new stations have been added, eight of which are in sector I (Kimbembi, 2009) and two in sector II (cave B_{26} and cave Muisi). However, in two (Kambu cave and Ebeya cave) of the eight new localities discovered (sector I), the presence of these blind fish is no longer observed. In short, at present these fish are observed only in ten caves, two of which are old.

The objective of this work is, on the one hand, to contribute, correct and complete Leleup and Heuts (1954), on the other hand, to encourage scientists and international institutions of biodiversity conservation to get involved in the safeguarding of this heritage, and to put at the disposal of decision makers, a set of data in order to reach their affective level, as for: - the threats that these natural reserves with defined goals, scientific, aesthetic, cultural and educational value, special reserves, these caves characterized by the presence of blind albino fish, species of endemic fish, *Caecobarbus geertsii*; and - the concern to have some of these caves inventoried on the list of world heritage properties. Because, to do nothing would lead ineluctably, in a more or less long term, to the loss of these ecosystems of great universal value.

This manual is structured in five chapters: the first chapter describes the study area, the second chapter presents general information on caves and *Caecobarbus geertsii*, the material and methods are presented in chapter three, the results and discussion are presented in chapter four, and in chapter five an outline of the structure of the Mbanza-Ngungu cave biosphere reserve is proposed.

CHAPTER I: STUDY AREA, THE TERRITORY OF MBANZA-NGUNGU

1.1 Physical environment

1.1.1 Geographical location of the explored region (Fig.1)

Kongo-Central is one of the 26 provinces of the DRC, located west of Kinshasa, the capital. It is the only province in the country that provides access to the Atlantic Ocean via three major communication routes: the asphalt road, National Road No.[0] 1; the railroad and the river. These routes link Kinshasa to Muanda, via Matadi and Boma.

Mbanza-Ngungu is built on a mountain at an altitude of about 750 meters. The ridge of Mbanza-Ngungu extends continuously to the south, until the vicinity of Mbanza-Nsundi, where it reaches an altitude of 850 meters. At Kiasi-Kolo and Kiasi-Mankala, this ridge is cut by the very deep valley of the Kokosi, a tributary of the Kwilu River, which flows at an altitude of 650 meters. The Matadi-Kinshasa railroad line passes through this area.

North of Mbanza-Ngungu, the ridge meets the Bangu massif, a high plateau of 600 to 700 meters, which heads southwest and ends in a vertical slope north of Kimpese, in front of the Kwilu valley.

The caves that were the subject of our study are located in the southeastern part of the city of Mbanza-Ngungu, in the Boko sector (Fig.1).

The territory of Mbanza-Ngungu is located at 14° 55' 25" east longitude and 5° 18' 30" south latitude. To the north, it is bordered by the Congo River and the territory of Luozi; to the south, by Angola; to the east, by the territory of Madimba and to the west, by the territory of Songololo.

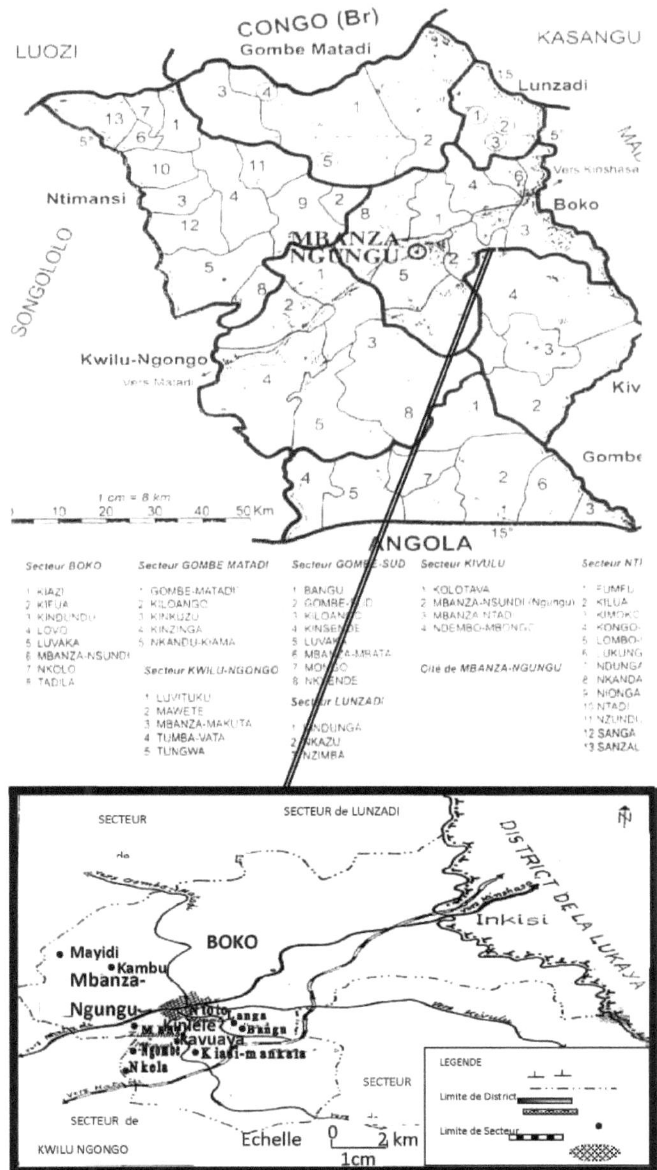

Fig. 1: Geographic location of the explored region (from the Geographic Institute, 1962)

1.1.2 Relief (after Quinif, 1985)

The region gathers a great diversity of karstic forms, characteristic of the evolution of a limestone massif under a tropical climate. The Mbanza-Ngungu ridge, which extends from Mbanza-Ngungu to Kiasi and Kolo, is the least typically karstic relief. Numerous ravines cut into the hillsides. There are few places where the limestone outcrops, which is most often hidden under the covering sands or under a mantle of alterites.

1.1.3 Hydrography

This entire region is part of the Congo River basin (Fig. 2). The southeast ridge of Mbanza-Gungu separates it from the Inkisi basin to the east and the Kwilu basin to the west. This ridge is the source of many spring heads that feed these two basins.

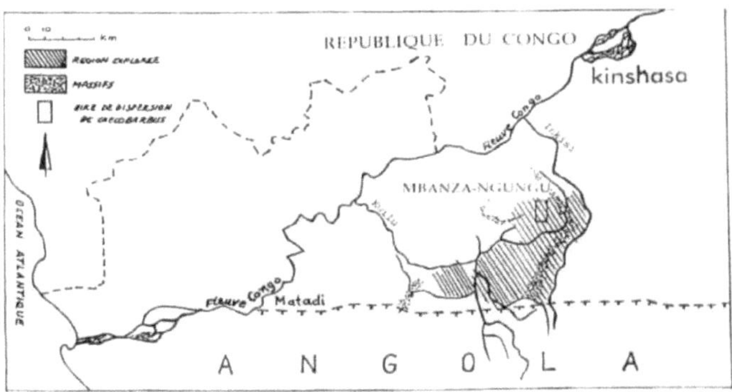

Fig.2 : Hydrography of the Mbanza-Ngungu region (after Heuts and Leleup, 1954)

1.1.4 Geology (after Quinif, 1985)

The geological structure (Fig.3) of the region is simple. The layers are almost horizontally stratified, on a base formed essentially of detrital rocks (quartzites, schists, conglomerates etc.), schisto-calcareous and schisto-sandstone formations and sand.

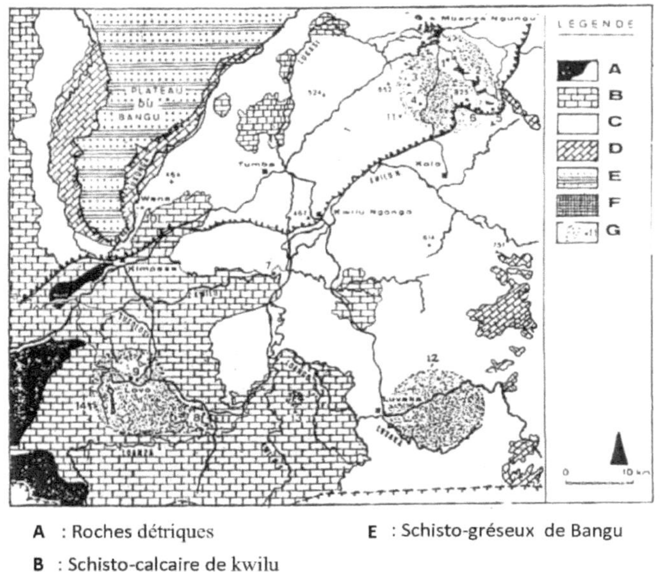

A	: Roches détriques	E	: Schisto-gréseux de Bangu
B	: Schisto-calcaire de kwilu		
C	: Schisto-calcaire de lukunga	F	: Sables tertiaires sous forme de
D	: Schisto-calcaire de Bangu	G	: Reliefs karstiques, crête de Mbanza-Ngungu

Fig.3 : Geological structure of the Mbanza-Ngungu area (after Quinif, 1985)

1.1.5 Climate

The territory of Mbanza-Ngungu has a tropical climate characterized by two seasons: a rainy season and a dry season. The rainy season extends from mid-October to mid-May. It is interspersed by a short dry season, from mid-January to mid-March. The dry season lasts about five months and goes from mid-May to mid-October.

According to Koppen's criteria (Gillain, 1953), the climate of the Mbanza-Ngungu territory is of the Aw type[5]. This climate allows the population to grow crops in season A (from mid-October to mid-January), season B (from mid-March to mid-May) and season C (from mid-May to mid-August).

In the Mbanza-Ngungu area, the average temperature is 24.4 °C; April is the hottest month with an average temperature of 26.1 °C while July is the coldest with an average temperature of 22.3 °C.

1.1.6 Vegetation

The vegetation of the region is characterized, on the one hand, by a shrubby savanna, dominated by *Psorospermum febrifugum* Spach, *Anthocleista schweinfurthii* Gily and *Hymenocardia acida* Tul. and, on the other hand, by a secondary forest with *Musanga cecropioides* R. Br. which most often surrounds the villages. In some places, such as the entrances to caves or old abandoned villages, heliophilous species such as *Myrianthus arboreus* P. Beauv. and *Milicia excelsa* (Welw.) Benth.

1.1.7 Location of the caves

According to Heuts and Leleup (1954), in the Cataract district, the caves are located in two administrative entities: the territory of Mbanza-Ngungu and that of Songololo (Fig. 4).

The territory of Mbanza-Ngungu includes two zones (I and II) of cave concentration. The territory of Songololo constitutes the zone III. Our investigations were concentrated first in zone I located in the administrative sector of Boko and recently in zone II located in the administrative sector of Gombe-Sud, both in the territory of Mbanza-Ngungu, district of Cataracts, Central Kongo Province, 150 km west of Kinshasa and 210 km east of Matadi.

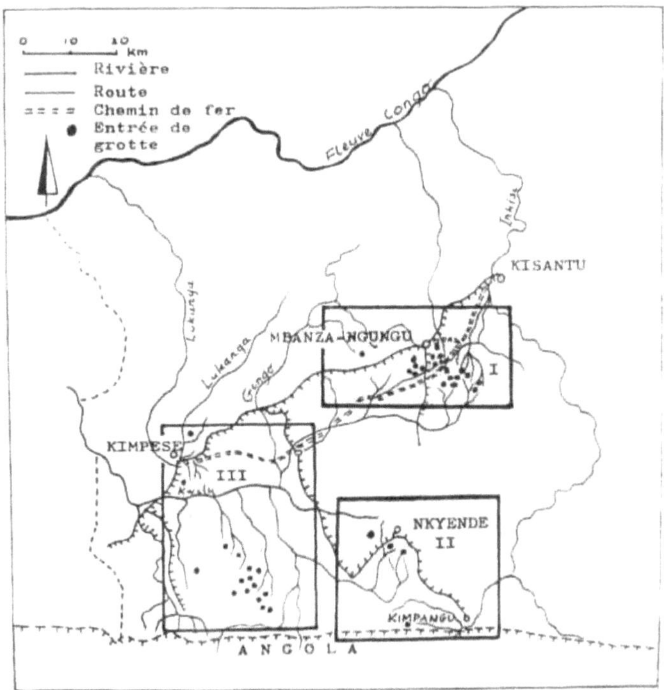

Fig. 4: Location of caves in the Cataract District (after Heuts and Leleup, 1954)

I.2 Human Environment: Administrative Subdivisions and Population

The province of Central Kongo, whose capital is Matadi, has an area of 53,920 km^2 . It comprises three single divisions [Bas-Fleuve (9,980 km^2), Cataractes (24,611 km2), and Lukaya (16,019 km2)] and two urban districts (Boma and Matadi). The Cataractes division is subdivided into three territories: the territory of Songololo (8,190 km2), the territory of Luozi (7,512 km2) and the territory of Mbanza-Ngungu (8,989 km2).

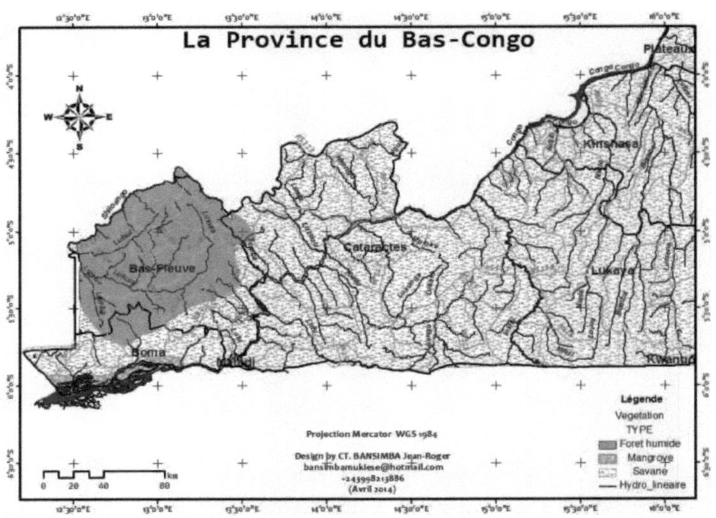

Fig. 5: Map of the province of Central Kongo (formerly Bas-Congo)

Table 1. Cataract District, Administrative Subdivision

Parameters	Territories			
	Luozi	Mbanza-Ngungu	Songololo	Total
Sector	10	7	5	22
Cities	1	4	2	7
Groups	37	47	13	97
Villages	535	785	411	1.731
Population	168.848	360.122	213.956	742.926
Area (in km $)^2$	7.512	8.989	8.190	24.691
Density (per km2)	23	57	21	

Sources: Annual reports from the territories of Luozi, Mbanza-Ngungu and Songololo (fiscal year 2005).

The population is unevenly distributed among the three territories, with 48.5 percent of the district's population living in Mbanza-Ngungu territory. Table 2 shows the administrative subdivision and the population of the territory of Mbanza-Ngungu.

Table 2. Territory of Mbanza-Ngungu, sectors and population

Sectors	Groups	Villages	Area (in km $)^2$	Population
1. Boko	8	174	1.438	99.259
2.Gombe-Matadi	5	87	1.875	40.248
3. South Gombe	8	239	1.3459	70.704
4. Kivulu	4	72	1.059	61.251
5. Kwilu-Ngongo	5	140	1.648	36.109
6. Lunzadi	3	55	260	14.589
7. Ntimansi	13	123	1.360	37.962
TOTAL	46	890	8.989	360.122

Source: Annual report of the Mbanza-Ngungu territory, (fiscal year 2005).

Table 2 shows that the population is concentrated in two sectors (Boko and Gombe-Sud) where the caves are located and are subject to strong human pressure.

CHAPTER II: GENERALITIES ON CAVES AND *CAECOBARBUS GEERTSII*.

The degradation of the biophysical environment is taking on worrying dimensions in Central Kongo Province. The galloping demographic pressure, the lack of rational management of natural resources and the resulting impasse constitute factors of this degradation. This is evidenced by the widespread deforestation that extends from Kasangulu (Lukaya Division), which is in danger of becoming an annex to the city of Kinshasa, to the coastal area of Moanda (Bas-fleuve Division).

The destruction of the natural environment results in the reduction of biodiversity and their habitats. And, doing nothing, the sustainability over time of all these species (animal and plant) dependent on these habitats is uncertain.

11.1 Caves : Definition and values

According to Ginet and Decou (1977), the cave is a volume of restricted space enveloped by an immense layer of inert rock on all sides except at the level of its entrance, which is often of minimal dimensions.

Leysbeth (1958) defines a cave as a more or less horizontal underground cavity. While the vertical one is called abyss or chasm.

Among the values of the Mbanza-Ngungu caves, we can cite: political value, sociological value, educational value, scientific value and economic value.

The political value results from the fact that caves can foster international relations, both at the individual and inter-state levels.

The sociological value results from the fact that caves meet a human need for relaxation in nature, increasingly felt in the urban world. The visitor relearns to respect nature from which he is isolated by his urban environment. For the rural people, the caves have served not only

as places of refuge during the colonial invasion, but also to the capture of Megachiropters, extinct around 1900 as a result of their unrestrained hunting.

The ecological value of the Mbanza-Ngungu caves is explained by the fact that they serve as a groundwater reservoir.

The educational value can be understood through outreach efforts to engage the curiosity and interest of visitors. They will come to understand the importance of conservation and appreciate the scientific value of the caves.

Scientific value: all scientific progress has its origin in the observation of nature. Although caves are very small ecological islands, they are nevertheless places of great biological importance that make them potential reserves for the preservation of biodiversity.

Economic value: caves, with atypical development (Mallet, pers. com. 2004) or development that requires little investment, generate revenue (access fees, lodging, food and profits for transporters) from tourism.

For market gardeners, these cavities are used to exploit the deposits of chiropteran guano, used as organic fertilizer.

The value of existence: it is the value of being, i.e. a value not linked to use. It is a value attached to the simple fact of knowing that a precious good exists in the region.

The patrimonial value which is a value attached to the legacies, to the descendants for its uses and not uses.

11.1.1 Formation of a cave (after Leysbeth, 1958)

The formation of a cave in a limestone soil is due to a chemical destruction of the limestone rocks by rainwater. These waters exert on the limestone rocks a double work: a physical work which is the erosion (degradation or wear of the earth's crust, produced by the atmospheric agents, in particular water) and a chemical work, the corrosion (dissolution of limestone due to the runoff water).

The earth's crust was once a molten mass that cooled, at least on its outer rim, and in this way the earth's crust was formed. This cooling was accompanied by the formation of cracks and fissures more or less deep.

It is during the Pliocene, the last period of the Tertiary Era, that rainfall was exceptionally abundant. It is obvious that during this period, water exerted with the most intensity its physical work of erosion. Water penetrated the cracks in the bark. It caused landslides and ceiling collapses. The water, which continued to flow, carried this debris downwards, creating sometimes narrow corridors, sometimes real underground rooms whose dimensions are sometimes surprising and frightening.

The chemical work of water is corrosion. Corrosion is the property of water to dissolve limestone into carbonate of lime. In the case of caves, another element intervenes and makes the corrosion much more active, it is the carbon dioxide (CO_2). Thus the reaction is as follows (Heuts and Leleup, 1954): $CaCO_3 + CO_2 + H_2O <-> Ca(HCO)_{32}$ (soluble calcium bicarbonate)

As a result, the carbonate of lime, one of the components of limestone, is deposited in concretion, on the ceiling, as on the floor. The water seeping from the ceiling brings, drop after drop, a tiny quantity of $Ca(HCO)_{32}$ which settles and, after some years, forms a kind of cone, attached to the ceiling by its base and whose point is directed downwards: it is the stalactite (Fig. 6). This is the stalactite (Fig. 6). It is crossed in the middle by a small, very narrow channel that ends up being blocked. It is by there that the water, charged with limestone, passes to fall on the floor of the cave, and it forms the stalagmite (Fig.7). The pointed end of this one is turned upwards.

Fig. 6: Stalactite (Wongo cave)

Fig.7 : Stalagmite in a pond (Dimba cave)

Sometimes the stalactite and the stalagmite meet, forming a real column in the middle of the cave. This column can be an obstacle to the passage during the exploration.

11.1.2 Ecological conditions

Tropical caves provide much the same ecological conditions for living things as those in temperate regions. Caves, inhabited by troglobitic species, are characterized by a complex of physicochemical and biotic factors (Heuts and Leleup, 1954).

The Darkness

Among the factors that characterize the caves, the darkness is the most striking.

It is impossible to explore a cave without artificial light sources. This darkness (Heuts and Leleup, 1954) seems to play as important a role as other factors in the survival of the eggs of *Caecobarbus geertsii* and the juvenile stages and thus on the maintenance of the species.

The Temperature

In caves, temperature variations are always strongly attenuated compared to the outside environment.

Generally speaking, the temperature of a cave is equal to the average annual temperature of the area. This rule also applies to the Bas-Congo, where the average annual temperature is 22.9 °C. Air temperatures in the caves range from 22° C to 24° C.

Relative humidity

It is generally accepted that the high and constant relative humidity of the underground domain is of paramount importance for the development of fauna. Only humid caves are populated. The dry caves are practically azoic. The microclimate, where troglobitic animals live, seems to be close to saturation in humidity. It can exceed 95%. In the Wongo cave, at a depth of ± 20 m, the relative humidity reaches 90%.

The Origin of the Waters

Three quarters of the rainwater that falls on the earth's surface evaporates. Only a quarter of the water infiltrates the ground. The water percolating into the ground will form resurgences and underground streams. Ponds and puddles, found on the floor, originate either from rainwater that rushes in during the rainy season, or from seepage or small resurgences. These pools, which communicate with each other during the rainy season, can be discontinuous during the dry season.

Chemical Factors

The nature of the limestone, the chemical composition of the water and air, in the subterranean domain, have never been considered to play a causal role in the maintenance and genesis of the cave fauna. However, it would be important to pay some attention to the chemical conditions that characterize limestone caves. Indeed, some caves, whose entrances are located on the hillsides, are fed by rainwater. These biotopes differ considerably from the typical underground aquatic environment where pools and puddles are fed only by seepage or small resurgences. The chemical reactions that take place in the cave water when it enters the cave naturally affect the composition of the air: the carbon dioxide, which the runoff water has enriched during its passage through the soil layers, escapes into the underground atmosphere.

Biotic Factors

The total absence of green plants is a biotic factor that characterizes the caves. It has for remarkable consequences, the accumulation of carbonic gas.

11.1.3 Dangers and precautions

No research that involves underground exploration can be undertaken without incurring risks. Various precautions must be taken. It is not advisable to go alone into a rarely visited or unexplored cave. You must have the appropriate equipment. A lighting system is necessary to avoid falling into chasms or getting lost in one of the branches, especially when returning from exploration.

For a cave visited for the first time, the contribution of a rope, serving as a telephone wire, is mandatory in order to stay in contact with the outside. It is also this rope which will facilitate the exit.

Finally, you must:

- inform the village population of the duration of the exploration;
- have clothing that protects you when you get down on your stomach;
- Avoid walking on slippery rocks, especially in a cave where a river flows;
- Be aware of head, knee, hand and shoulder injuries that can result from rough contact with the arch and floor. Helmets and rubber pads should be worn;
- a personal discipline which consists in not engaging in certain chokes, with impossibility of turning or going back;
- avoid objects in pockets or on belts that could cause injury.

II.1.4 State of research in caving

For Alfred Martel, inventor of speleology and defender of nature, speleological expeditions seek to respond to the following two aspects: science and sport (Céline, 2000).

As far as science is concerned, the data obtained from the exploration and study of underground cavities can be used for the conservation and protection of a set of well-defined elements related to archaeology, geology, hydrology, zoology or anthropology. On the other hand, the discovery of cavernous wonders and this new sport, which consists in following the corridors of a cave, in descending in a chasm with the help of a ladder or a rope, are part of the satisfaction of the needs of the man.

In the present state of our knowledge, scientific considerations in this field can be seen in several ways, notably from the archaeological and biological angles. In archaeology, for example, 700 fragments of Old Testament manuscripts have been found in the caves of Qumran, an archaeological site in Palestine. The engravings and cave paintings of the Congo caves have interested Breuil (1952), in Katanga, and De Munck and Raymarkers (1961) and Mandjuma (1984), in the Lower Congo, where the historical aspects have been approached in particular by Mortelmans and Monteyne (1962) and by Raymarkers and Van Moorsel (1964). De Maret (1986) was interested in pottery in the Dimba and Ngovo caves.

Speleological expeditions by Heuts and Leleup (1954) and by Quinif (1985) in the Bas-Congo revealed the characteristics and topography of some caves.

Regarding the biodiversity of cave fauna, it is recognized that some caves are shelters sought after by a specific fauna (troglobia or troglophile). This is the case of *Neotoma*, a genus of Rodentia, which is adapted to cave life in the U.S.A., and whose eyes are in danger of disappearing. Systematic research has led to the discovery of other *Neotoma*, in Madagascar, Eritrea and Katanga (Leysbeth, 1958).

Data on the cave fauna are rare. However, the cave fauna of France (Jeannel, 1926) has been studied. According to De Broyer (2005a), in Europe, the underground fauna counts only one stygobian vertebrate: the Proteus, an amphibian Urodele, endemic of the underground rivers of Slovenia, Croatia, Bosnia and the region of Trieste in Italy. It is of great patrimonial interest, because besides the adaptive traits to the subterranean life (depigmentation, disappearance of the eyes, slowing down of the development and delayed sexual maturity up to 15 years), it has preserved some primitive traits that the Amphibians possessed before conquering the continents and the aerial life by the metamorphosis

According to Eigenmann (1909), a number of species of blind fish are closely related to epigean species, possessing eyes and generally occupying the same hydrological system. His theory is to assume that all cave fishes would have started out as river fishes with eyes. During the process of formation of the valleys; these rivers would have progressively eroded the softest parts of their bed, especially the limestone parts, thus giving birth to underground streams.

In Africa and more precisely in Madagascar, lists of cave fauna (Invertebrates and Vertebrates) have been established by Hutcheon (1995) and Walters (1996).

In R.D. Congo, the general aspect of the cave fauna of the Belgian Congo had been defined by Leleup (1956).

As for the interest in discovering the wonders of nature, we note the development of underground tourism and the attraction of this new sport which consists in following the corridors of a cave. Indeed, in every field, what is unknown or unexplored attracts in an irresistible way.

From the point of view of their form, Leysbeth (1958) distinguishes the caves of the Congo whose exploration did not give yet sensational discoveries, of those having very long courses; let us quote for example: the record caves of Carlsbad in Mexico with 50 km of length; the cave of Pierre de saint Martin, in France, with 1.100 m of depth and the giant cave, in Italy, with a room of 138 m of height.

Tourism engineering in the karst domain is of interest to several countries, including Switzerland (www.grottes.ch/, 2005); France, including the Lascaux caves (www.culture.fr/arcnat/lascaux/f/, 2004); the Médous caves (www.grottes-medous.com/, 2005); and the Betharram caves (www.betharram.com/, 2005).

Finally, in our country, speleology is still at the stage of census. Apart from the caves in Central Kongo and those reported in the limestone outcrops in the Upemba National Park by Kabala (1976), there are others mentioned by the Ministry of the Environment, Nature Conservation and Tourism (1996): twenty-six caves in Mount Hoyo in Ituri; caves of volcanic origin in Kivu, Katana and Goma; the Salonga cave in Kasai and finally in Katanga, the caves of Mpitashi, Lufundu with an underground lake and Kando, which is a habitat for blind fish have been listed.

With regard to the protection and conservation of underground ecosystems, according to UNESCO (1972), the caves that have been included in the World Heritage List were inscribed on the basis of six cultural and four natural criteria.

It appears from our analysis that the investigations dedicated to the systemic study of the cave biodiversity for their conservation in our country are non-existent.

From the above, it seemed imperative to review our consideration in the field of cave biodiversity that deserves to be safeguarded. For some of these caves (Kiamvu, Lukatu, Ngovo, Nkienge and Muisi) meet certain criteria for selection as world heritage properties.

Since the Mbanza-Gungu caves are part of the rural world, and since the latter is a complex system, it is important that it be treated in its complexity and in its entirety, taking into account the interactions between the different components.

In our opinion, the most appropriate way is the integration of some areas into the network of UNESCO biosphere reserves or the inclusion of some caves that meet the criteria on the list of world heritage properties.

Indeed, in the current state of affairs, the caves in the territory of Mbanza-Ngungu will not be able to persist for much longer, not only because of the multiple negative impacts resulting from the activities of local and foreign populations on the sites, to the point that the insufficiently controlled use of the land, where the caves are located, has a negative impact on them. But above all because of the possible extension of the town of Mbanza-Ngungu on a radius of 11 km.

Establishing such a balance is particularly difficult, so we will strive to protect the fragile and threatened cryptic system by seeking international recognition.

The support sought can come from UNESCO, either by including some caves on the list of World Heritage properties, or by requesting the same institution to recognize the macro-system as a biosphere reserve. In either case, within the framework of the rural system concept under consideration, UNESCO plays the role of an external catalyst.

It may happen that such international recognition cannot be obtained. In this case the Congolese state itself must be involved.

In any case, the key to success in the long run lies in the involvement of the population and its leaders in the management and safeguarding of the exceptional natural resources that characterize their territory. Without this conscious participation of the population, there will be no desired sustainability. Only mesological education can lead to a responsible involvement of the population in the conservation of the cryptic system.

Indeed, some sites of great natural beauty and inestimable value, which man cannot recreate, are included in the list of world heritage properties. And, during the 17ᵉ session of the Convention on cultural and natural heritage, adopted on November 22, 1972 in Paris, UNESCO recognized the importance of caves as cultural and natural heritage, especially in its articles 1er and 2^{e} .

Its first article states: "Monuments, architectural works, sculptures or monumental paintings, elements or structures of an archaeological nature, inscriptions, caves and groups of elements, which are of outstanding universal value from the point of view of history, art or science, shall be considered as cultural heritage".

The second article states: "The following are considered as natural heritage: geological formations and strictly delimited areas constituting the habitat of threatened animal and plant species, which are of outstanding universal value from the point of view of science, conservation or natural beauty".

II. 2 Status of the question on *Caecobarbus geertsii*

Animals that live in caves often attract the attention of biologists. This is the case of the blind fish in the caves of Mbanza-Ngungu which have been the subject of several investigations.

It was in 1912 that Geerts collected in one of the caves around Mbanza-Ngungu, the first specimens of a blind fish of the family Cyprinidae (Leleup, 1956). This small fish was described by Boulenger (1921) under the name *Caecobarbus geertsii*.

The diagnosis of Boulenger (*op.cit.*) has been completed by some authors. Pellegrin (1926) mentioned that *Caecobarbus geertsii does* not possess any vestige of eyes: "these organs, he said, have completely disappeared, and one does not find even a trace of them by lifting the skin >>. The fish is entirely discolored in its living state. Its hue is white, as is the rule for cave-dwelling animals. Its very thin and very soft scales do not show any striation. It is still Pellegrin (1930) who revealed the arrangement of its pharyngeal teeth in two rows and the presence of divergent striations of its scales. According to Petit (1938), its scales present circuli, in general and radiali almost always more numerous in the higher half of the scale.

In contrast, Poll (1953) observed that light had an effect on the pigmentation of a specimen of *Caecobarbus geertsii*:<< living in a dimly lit aquarium, he wrote, it had become pigmented over time in a very obvious manner. The scales of the back and flanks offered melanophores as did the dorsal and caudal fins."

About the complete disappearance of its eyes, Gerard (1936), through a histological study, came to different conclusions: << on external examination, the head of *Caecobarbus* presents at the place normally occupied by the orbit, a broad shallow depression, covered by fatty clusters which fill the bony cavities of the face. It is in one of them that the eyes are deeply buried.

Its pituitary gland has also been the subject of a histological study. According to Olivereau and Herlant (1954), the examination of the sagittal median sections of its pituitary gland shows the classical large regions of the pituitary gland of the Teleosts: pars anterior, middle glandular region, pars intermédia and pars nervosa.

As for its ethology in aquarium, according to Petit and Besnard (1937), *Caecobarbus geertsii* would be absolutely indifferent to light. On the other hand, the phototropic reactions carried out by Thines (1952) testified to the existence of an extra-ocular photo sensitivity in this species. According to Thinès and Legrain (1973), the alarm substance determines in this species a food exploration directed towards the bottom.

Addressing the aspect of its ecology, Heuts (1951) initiated the study of the condition factor of the six populations (B5, B7, B11, B15, B16 and B20), among which, the population B15 had presented a negative allometry.

Concerning cytology, the number of its chromosomes is known ($2n = 50$) thanks to the study of the epithelium of its gill by Vervoort (1980). These chromosomes are divided into three groups: 12 medium, 28 submedium and 10 subternal.

As for its distribution, according to Heuts and Leleup (1954), this species is located in the lower reaches of the Congo basin at 5° south latitude and 15° east longitude.

Finally, it is known that *Caecobarbus geertsii is the* subject of aquarium fish and protection. Indeed, Poll (1951 and 1953) writes: << *Caecobarbus geertsii* from the Thysville caves is an aquarium curiosity that will not be imported every day, as it is currently the only fish protected by law in D.R. Congo". Indeed, *Caecobarbus geertsii* is one of the fishes listed in Appendix II of CITES (M.E.C.N.P.F., 1998). It is a species classified "vulnerable" by the IUCN (Lévêque and Daget, 1984). However, according to Bensalem (1999), this listing should, in principle, promote the taking of concrete protection and management measures aimed at conserving and increasing these genetic resources threatened by extinction or depletion. This is not the case for the caves of

Mbanza-Ngungu, which are home to this species.

In order to fill this gap, we have sought to complete its area of occupation by new expeditions and to propose a management plan for the conservation of these ecosystems either by proposing this area as a protected area, namely a biosphere reserve (cluster) of the Mbanza-Ngungu caves; or by registering some caves as world heritage properties.

11.3 The need for wildlife conservation

It is also necessary to remember that animal species, considered today as without interest, according to our usual criteria, can be conserved because it could be useful to the man. Indeed, they can be called tomorrow, to play an important role in one or another field. For example, they can be used not only as laboratory animals to prepare vaccines and perform medical tests, but also as biological material *in situ* to deepen studies of certain biological aspects.

We are far from knowing all the possibilities that wild species can offer us, whose biology and ecology are still little known.

11.4 : Special aspects of fish conservation

For Mutambue (1999), the capture or disappearance of the last *Caecobarbus geertsii* would have less of an impact on those not concerned with nature conservation than the announcement of the massacre of the last white rhinoceros, *Ceratotherium simum* (Burchell, 1817). There are two main reasons for this. The first one is that the observation of fishes, in natural environment, is not easy (it is for blind fishes that live in caves with clear waters). It is much less than that of Mammals and Aves which are, therefore, better known to the public. The changes that affect their population and eventually their local disappearance often go unnoticed. Secondly, public opinion tends to minimize the dangers that threaten their habitats. The greatest dangers do not come from overfishing, but mainly from environmental modifications and pollution, the harmful effects of which are not always directly perceptible (Mutambue, 1999).

11.5 : Need for basic knowledge to justify protective measures

It is essential that the technical services responsible for nature conservation, with the help of specialists, work to collect and popularize documentation on endangered animal species.

According to Mutambue (1999), the most urgent data to be collected are faunal lists by region and distribution maps by species, which must be constantly updated. The second urgent need for nature conservation services is to elaborate "red books" that will allow them to evaluate the impact of industrial, agricultural or tourist projects that are submitted to them.

The World Union for Nature (IUCN, 2001) has elaborated a classification of the threatened species based on the criteria not only on the reduction of their population, in its diverse forms, but also on their geographical distribution, whether it is the zone of occurrence or the zone of occupation. As far as we are concerned, it is known that *Caecobarbus geertsii* is included in the red list of the IUCN on August 1, 1996, as a vulnerable species (Lévêque et *al.*, 1984). According to the IUCN (2001), a vulnerable species is a species facing a high risk of extinction in the wild. This implies *ipsofacto* the protection of the habitat of *Caecobarbus geertsii.*

11.6 The Fish, *Caecobarbus geertsii* Boulenger, 1921

We introduce here the Blindbeard, which is the focus of this document, whose fundamental objective is its protection, following a systemic approach.

11.6.1 Systematic position and distribution of Caecobarbus geertsii (after Nelson, 1994)

- Class Actinopterygii ;
- Subclass Neopterygii ;
- Teleostei Division;
- Super-order Ostariophysi ;
- Order Cypriniformes ;
- Family Cyprinidae ;
- Genus: *Caecobarbus* Boulenger, 1921 ;
- Species: *Caecobarbus geertsii* Boulenger, 1921 ;
- Kikongo name : Nzonzi.

In the caves of the Mbanza-Ngungu area, the family Cyprinidae is represented by two genera and two species: *Caecobarbus geertsii* (Fig. 8) and *Garra congoensis* Poll, 1958.

II.6.2 Presentation of the species, Caecobarbus geertsii Boulenger, 1921

Caecobarbus geertsii is a fish with a laterally compressed body covered with cycloid scales. According to Gerard (1936), it is not only a blind fish, but it is also a true albino. The fin formulas are as follows:

- the dorsal fin D: II (III)/7-8 ;
- the anal fin A: III/5 ;
- the pectoral fin P :I/11-15;
- the ventral fin V : I/7-8.

The lateral line consists of 28-29 scales.

Fig. 8.1: *Caecobarbus geertsii* captured

Fig. 8.2 : *Caecobarbus geertsii*, measurements

II. 6.3 Distribution

In Africa, Roberts (1975) distinguishes 10 ichthyological provinces, including the Zaire region (including lakes Kivu and Tanganika) where, according to Teugels and Guéran (1994), three hydrographic zones are usually distinguished. The first, which corresponds to Lualaba, goes from the source of the Congo River to Kisangani, and is called the Upper Congo. The second zone goes from Kisangani to Kinshasa, it is the middle Congo. The third zone or maritime reach goes from Kinshasa to Matadi, it is the Bas-Congo.

The distribution area of *Caecobarbus geertsii* is located in the third zone of the Congo River basin, more precisely in the vicinity of the city of Mbanza-Ngungu.

A unique species, *Caecobarbus geertsii* is a known form from the lower reaches of the Congo Basin. It is found in the caves of Mbanza-Ngungu (5° 18' S, 14° 50' E),

According to Heuts and Leleup (1954), the geographical distribution of this species is limited to the Mbanza-Ngungu-Kiasi high plateau, south of the city of Mbanza-Ngungu.

Blind species of the family Cyprinidae are also found in Asia, such as *Puntius microps* (Günther, 1868). In Somalia, they are represented by *Eilichthys microphtalmus* Pellegrin, 1929 (Hubbs, 1938).

III: METHODS AND MATERIALS

Methodologically, our approach includes three steps: deduction, data analysis and induction.

111.1 Boundary and identified elements

Our study was conducted from January 2000 to July 2005. For reasons of proximity, we initially chose the caves located southeast of Mbanza-Ngungu. Because of the poor condition of the roads and the rains, two periods for visiting the caves were selected: the short dry season (mid-January to mid-March) and the long dry season (mid-May to mid-October).

Among the elements that were identified and counted, the caves (an emerging quality of the land) caught our attention because of their interest and their state of degradation. After 2005, the work continues. It consists not only in a continuous monitoring of the sites with *Caecobarbus geertsii* in sector I but also in the exploration of the caves in sector II.

Documentation and listening to the population

Collection of socio-economic data

During this stage, based on bibliographic data and information from the tourism department of the Cataractes district, the work consisted of visits to the investigation areas, with the aim of establishing a climate of trust with the population. Participatory surveys were carried out, based on an interview scheme covering socio-economic characteristics and the production sub-system.

Participatory observation

The technique of participatory observation was used to understand the daily life and socio-cultural practices of the target population in relation to the caves. This allowed us to describe the different contexts: ecological, sociological, political and cultural of the community. The purpose

was to make a first contact with the village chief, to negotiate the customary rights and to agree on the stay for the exploration of the caves, located in his entity.

Collection of technical data on the state of knowledge about caves

In order to establish the balance of knowledge of these biotopes, data relating to the inventory and management of these ecosystems were collected.

Since the activities in which the population engages refer to their perceptions, attitudes and practices, the most appropriate approach is that of the target group. The technical data focused on the assessment of the knowledge of the cave biodiversity of the region explored. This knowledge assessment relates to the location and management of caves in the area. Each group consisted of eight to ten people, belonging to the same social category and having the same characteristics in terms of gender, age and level of education.

The interviews allowed us to inventory the caves, to locate them and to identify their remarkable elements.

As for the aspects, related to the management of the caves, they consisted in :

- to identify the actors, the users, the mode of management of the caves, the conflicts of use and the rivalries of interests;
- Establish the constraints, both natural and real estate;
- to highlight the traditions in the way of protection;
- Assess the impacts of historical and current human activities and the impacts of current and potential human pressure;
- To collect the opinions and wishes of the participants on the project as well as their involvement in the implementation of the different stages of the project. Individual interviews were conducted with traditional chiefs, women, military and political-administrative authorities and NGO leaders.

111.2 Analysis of data in their dynamic interactions

Data analysis was done through:

- to the four concepts of systemic analysis (concept of interaction, concept of totality, concept of organization and concept of complexity);
- the general laws of systems (law of relationship with the environment, law of conservation of systems, law of need for variety and law of evolution of systems);
- to the rural system concept (Maldague et *al.*, 1997).

111.3 Inductive phase

Taking into account the poor basic conditions of rural development and the dynamism of the rural population, as well as the production system of this area, the way to solve the problems of this macro-system is to propose this area as a biosphere reserve or to include some caves in the list of world heritage properties. This may allow :

- to develop human resources, (by fighting against poverty and its causes);
- to achieve a rational management of natural resources, (by coupling environmental management and development);
- initiate a process of sustainable self-development.

111.4 In each village where the presence of a cave was detected, customary rights in kind or in cash were negotiated. In fact, in each case, protocol requires that the village chief be approached first. The latter can only authorize entry into one or another of the village's caves with the agreement of the three lineages that make up the clan that owns the proposed cave.

The visit of each site was possible only after invocation of the spirits of their ancestors, just at the entrance of the cave and under the presidency of the clan chief. The first visit only allowed us a summary exploration; it essentially allowed us to locate the caves.

A second or third visit was necessary, not only to make morphological observations and to take photographs, but also to proceed to the qualifying inventory of the animal species, infodicated to each cave, and to assure us, especially in the case of the caves crossed by a watercourse, of the presence or absence of the species *Caecobarbus geertsii.*

The chemical analysis of the water was carried out using a kit (Visicolor Eco).

111. 5 Cave exploration techniques

On each field trip, our equipment consisted of :

- a machete to cut a path to the entrance of the caves not frequented;
- a small hoe to create steps on slopes to easily reach the openings of the caves;
- a nylon rope (10 segments of 50 m length each) to ensure safety and to take measurements;

- plankton nets, mosquito nets, nylon nets and two mist nets for the capture of Crustaceans, Fish, Amphibians and Microchiroptera respectively;
- plastic bags and bottles for the conservation of the collected specimens;
- three Coleman lamps with a capacity of one liter of oil each to light the course;
- five flashlights, three of which are tubes (with rechargeable batteries) and two battery-operated headlamps (Petzl brand), for remote exploration (ceiling and walls);
- candles and matchboxes as emergency equipment, in case of light failure or to test the oxygenation of the environment;
- a camera;
- a G.P.S. (Global Positioning System) branded Geko 201 GARMIN, to record the geographical coordinates at the entrance of the caves which shelter the blind Barbus.

The actual exploration was facilitated by being accompanied by a local guide. From the entrance to the deep zone, passing through the penumbra zone, observations were made on the remarkable elements: the aspect of the floor and the walls; the height of the vault; the width and the length of the cavity; the impacts of the human pressure; the fauna, etc.

III.6 Techniques for capturing cave-dwelling species in galleries

The capture equipment included:

- a plankton net for the capture of Crustaceans;
- four landing nets, of small mesh, two of them with mosquito net, for the fishing of Fishes;
- two mist nets for the capture of Microchiroptera ;
- three plastic tweezers for the collection of other arthropods.

The capture consisted in collecting or noting the different animal species encountered along our route. The karst ecosystem includes a great diversity of biotopes. The organisms living in karst cavities and underground waters are not randomly distributed. They are organized in structured populations that respond to a certain number of ecological constraints.

Following the example of De Broyer (2005$_b$) the animals found were grouped into associations typical of the different zones:

- zone of entry of the cavities, still largely illuminated;
- dark, low-light area;
- deep zone where total darkness, a stable temperature and a very high humidity prevail permanently;
- parietal zone; that is to say the walls and the ceiling of the cave.

CHAPTER IV: RESULTS AND DISCUSSION: STATE OF THE CAVES

IV. 1 Inventory and characteristics of caves

The assessment of the knowledge of these cryptic ecosystems focused on the location of caves in the two administrative sectors (Boko sector and Gombe-sud sector).

IV.1.1 Caves in the Boko area

In the sector of Boko, we visited twenty-five caves (Fig. 9), but two caves however remained inaccessible, they are the Kadi cave (n^0 16) and the gas cave (n^0 25). Indeed, in the first one two streams (one epige and the other hypogeous) are engulfed, which makes its funnel slippery and in the second one the lack of adequate equipment did not allow the descent.

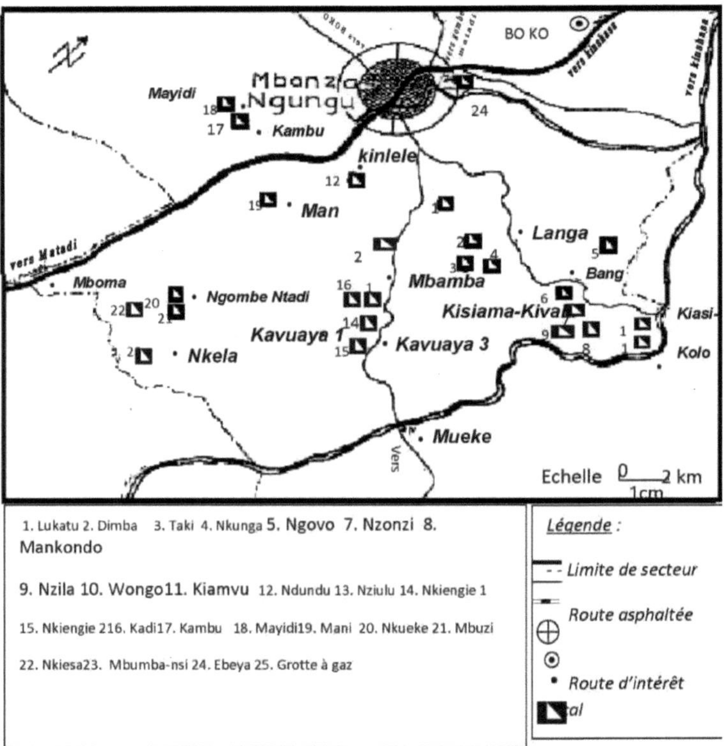

	Légende :
1. Lukatu 2. Dimba 3. Taki 4. Nkunga 5. Ngovo 7. Nzonzi 8. Mankondo	
9. Nzila 10. Wongo11. Kiamvu 12. Ndundu 13. Nziulu 14. Nkiengie 1	Limite de secteur
15. Nkiengie 216. Kadi17. Kambu 18. Mayidi19. Mani 20. Nkueke 21. Mbuzi	Route asphaltée
22. Nkiesa23. Mbumba-nsi 24. Ebeya 25. Grotte à gaz	Route d'intérêt

Fig. 9 Caves visited in the Boko area

IV. 1.1.1 Description of the caves

In this work only caves that shelter the blind fish were presented. In fact, some caves in the region do not contain this species of fish.

The caves were presented along five axes, starting from Mbanza-Ngungu (Kiasi-Mankala, Kavuaya, Ngombe-Ntadi, Kambu and Ebeya).

The Mbanza-N gungu-Kiasi-Mankala axis.

1° Grotte de Lukatu (n⁰ 1), 5° 17' 00. 0" south latitude; 14° 52' 26.8" east longitude.

Lukatu Cave, with a bare hill (Fig. 10), formerly called Randour Cave, is located to the southeast, 3 km from Mbanza-Ngungu. Its opening, hidden by a small grove, opens at an altitude of 685 m. According to Randour's estimate, the length of this cave is about 1,800 m (Heuts and Leleup, 1954).

Fig.10: Bare hill of the Lukatu cave

From the entrance (Fig.11), until about a hundred meters inside the cave, the vault is low, about one meter. It is a cave with resurgence and horizontal development. Its ceiling and its walls are made of limestone, while its floor is formed of shale.

Fig. 11 : Entrance to the Lukatu cave

More than 254 meters from the entrance, a resurgence emerges from the left side, whose waters flow into a 4-meter deep chasm. This chasm is 336 m from the entrance. Today, at the level of this chasm, not only the metal ladder that had been placed by Randour fell to the bottom of the chasm, but also around 1990, a gigantic stone fell from the vault (Fig.12), partially blocking the entrance of the chasm (Fig.13).

Fig. 12 : Stone fallen at the level of the chasm in the cave of Lukatu.

Fig.13 : Partial obstruction of the entrance to the chasm

During the rainy season, this cave receives all the runoff from the northeast hills. During this period, the cave is crossed by a river that disappears during the dry season, leaving only pools. In the latter, blind fish are easily observed. However in the framework of our continuous monitoring of cave biodiversity, since 2017, it was noted a silting of these pools. And, these fish are no longer observed.

2° Grotte de Ngovo (n° 5), latitude 55°18'42" south; 14°54'51" east longitude.

Ngovo Cave, formerly called Tordeur Cave, is located 1.5 km northeast of the village of Bangu, at an altitude of 748 m. Its opening, 4 m wide and 3 m high, is directed towards the south. The slope that leads to a large room is 60 m long. Its floor is made of yellowish clay. Two corridors leave this large room. One goes east and the other, which goes northwest, ends 50 m into a chasm. The ceiling of the hall, situated at about 30 m high, is made of shale. Clay mixed with guano forms the substrate of the floor. The eastern branch, 15 to 20 m wide, has two paths at 310 m that cross again at about 20 m. At this crossing point, a stalactite chamber can be observed (Fig. 14).

Fig. 14: Stalactites of the Ngovo cave

In this same branch, 500 m beyond the great hall, there is a waterfall (Fig.15) about fifty meters high.

These waters form an underground river (Fig. 16) whose depth (30-50 cm) increases as one moves away from the waterfall.

Fig. 15: Waterfall in the Ngovo cave

Fig. 16: Ngovo cave: underground river

The Ngovo cave or cave of the falls is the biotope that shelters the population of *Caecobarbus geertsii*. This population had not been reported by Heuts and Leleup (1954). The river thus formed flows in the northern direction. The influence of the flooding of an intermittent epigenetic stream to the southeast is felt in the groundwater of Ngovo Cave. Indeed, the waters, which are very clear during the dry season, become turbid during the rainy season between November and December. The arrival of the clay-laden water gives the rocky bottom a milky appearance, which makes the water turbid.

Since 2009, this cave has been developed atypically with the help of the Canadian Fund for Local Initiatives (CFLI) for biodiversity conservation and eco-tourism purposes.

3° Complex of Nzonzi and Mankondo caves

It is located in Kingo, a hamlet of the village of Bangu, at an altitude of 753 m.

a. Grotte de Nzonzi (n° 7) 5° 20' 23.3" south latitude; 14° 54' 14.8" east longitude.

The Nzonzi cave opens towards the north, but its cavity has a north-west orientation. It regularly receives the waters of two epigenetic streams which, at 3 m from the entrance, form a succession of two pools, one of which is 4 m in diameter and 50 cm deep, and the other, 3 m in diameter and 30 cm deep. These two pools constitute the habitat of blind fish. Their muddy bottom is explained by the contribution of various plant debris during the rainy season. After these pools, the height and width of the cave decrease significantly and end in a dead end at the. The ceiling of this cave is provided with several pointed stalactites. The length of the cave is about 40 m.

As the name suggests, "Nzonzi" means bearded. In this cave, the fish reach the entrance of the cave. This locality was not reported by Heuts and Leleup (1954).

    b.   **Mankondo Cave** (n^0 8), 5° 20' 22. 6" south latitude; 14° 54' 14.6" east longitude.

The cave of Mankondo, compared to that of Nzonzi, opens to the west, on the side of a banana plantation hill. It takes the form of a small funnel whose entrance, nearly 2 meters high, forms a slope that leads to a corridor 6 meters wide. These fish can be observed at the first pool. The ceiling is located at about ten meters. The floor and the walls are made of limestone. For about a hundred meters, the cave keeps a slight slope and goes towards the southwest. After that, the cave deviates to the north where it ends in a very deep abyss. This cave, which is traversed by a stream, would be the extension of the Nzonzi cave. This site was not also reported by Heuts and Leleup (1954).

4° Grotte de Kiamvu (n0 11), latitude 5°21'37" south; longitude 14°55'40" south.

The Kiamvu cave is located 4 km west of the Kiasi-Kolo station, more precisely in the village of Kiasi-Mankala, at an altitude of 630 m. The penumbra zone of this cave opens to the east of the village. This penumbra zone is characterized by the presence of several pools with blind fish and deep canyons. Its entrance, 2 m wide and 1.5 m high, receives the waters of an epigenetic stream that runs through the whole cave. This stream dries up in the dry season, but the cave keeps water thanks to resurgences.

After a course of nearly 1 km, the waters of this cave come out at the level of the bridge of the railway line Matadi-Kinshasa. The waters that flow out of this cave form a waterfall, at the bottom of which we can observe in the open air some *Caecobarbus geertsii*. Currently, we can say that the cave of Kiamvu is the richest in population of blind fish.

The Kavuaya axis.

In this axis three blind fish caves were recorded.

5° Grotte de Nziulu (n^0 13), 5° 19' 22.5" south latitude; 14° 51' 02.5" east longitude.

The Nziulu cave is located to the southwest, 600 m from the hamlet of Kavuaya 1, at an altitude of 528 m. It opens to the east, at the bottom of a deeply incised valley, with a steep and very slippery slope. It has two branches: one in the northeast direction and the other in the southwest direction. Both branches have a stream running through them.

In order to reach the horizontal gallery of the first branch, it is necessary to climb rocks of a height of 2 m. For a distance of 200 m, its floor is characterized by shallow canyons and pools. Beyond 200 m, a large hall opens up. After that, the cavity narrows down considerably.

The south-western branch is in fact only a continuation of the north-eastern branch. The dimensions of the cavity are up to 4 m high and 2 m wide. The ceiling is shaped like a two-slope roof. The substratum on which the stream flows is made up of sand and gravel. This branch has pools and communicates with the outside through two chasms, one of which is located at 60 m and the other at 180 m from the entrance to the northeast branch. Nziulu Cave is also a new blind fish cave not recorded by Heuts and Leleup (1954).

6° Complex of caves of Nkiengie

The caves of Nkiengie form a complex of two caves: Nkiengie 1 or Nkolo-kolo, Nkiengie 2. They open south of Kavuaya 3, at an altitude of 543 m, at 5° 19' 90.2" south latitude, 14° 50' 37.1" east longitude.

a. Cave of Nkiengie 1 (n° 14)

The cave of Nkiengie 1 opens to the north-east at 20m from the cave Nkiengie 2. To reach its opening, we had to create some steps. Its entrance is 15 m high and 7 m wide. The floor is strewn with gravel. In its inner area, there is a big stalagmite, behind which there is a pool of blind fish. At this level, the corridor narrows before widening. The main cavity of this cave is blocked by a broken stalactite. The breaking of this stalactite has caused a chasm which puts the cave in communication with the outside.

b. Cave of Nkiengie 2 (n° 15)

The Nkiengie 2 cave comprises in turn two branches: the northeast branch and the southwest branch. At 75 m from the entrance of the south-west branch, a resurgence flows. The floor is made of limestone concretions. The left wall is strewn with hollows. This branch opens out again, 300 m from the entrance. Unlike the south-western branch, the floor of the north-eastern branch is strewn with pebbles. Its course is choked at 53 m from the entrance. Then, the corridor suddenly becomes a large lounge. And at 250 m, where this cavity ends, we observe, on the ceiling, a large stalactite and on the floor, a pool (Fig. 17) with blind fish, 4 m in diameter.

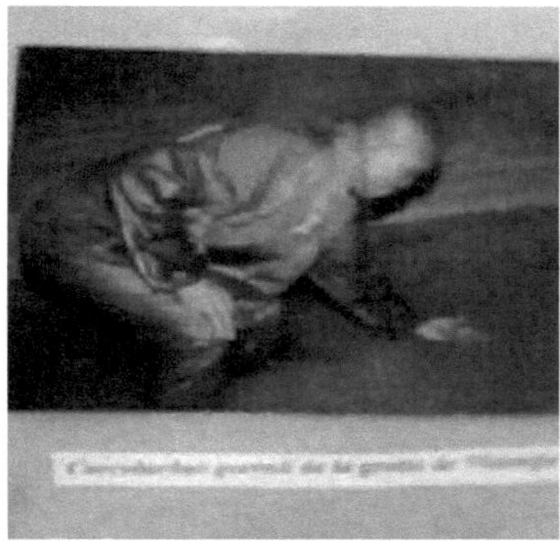

Fig.17: Nkiengie 2 cave: *Caecobarbus geertsii* pond

The Nkiengie cave complex had reported blind fish as a biotope (Heuts and Leleup, 1954).

7° Vungu cave, 5°19'2.2" south latitude; 14°51'55" east longitude.

The 2017 monitoring expedition revealed east of the village of Ntandalanga, about three km away, the presence of a cave Vungu cave the presence of blind fish. This cave does not look like a cave in the strict sense but rather a kind of crack that is visible at the surface with a "pool" at the bottom of which *Caecobarbus* can be observed.

This site was not reported by Heuts and Leleup (1954).

The Kambu axis

It includes a single cave.

8° Kambu cave (n° 17), 5°15'29.4" south latitude; 14°48'50.00" east longitude.

Kambu Cave is located west of the village of the same name, at an altitude of 602 m. Over a distance of 55 m, the vault is low, about 70 cm. The cave is traversed by an epigenetic stream (Ntembele) which has its source near the village of Luvaka. This stream forms a river whose waters are lost in the Tiki valley before flowing into the Kambu cave. The floor of this cave is made of pebbles, yellowish clay and gravel. At 500 m from the entrance, the corridor forms an abrupt bend in the west-east direction. The width of the gallery is about 5 m. The ceiling is at about 20 meters. The distance covered is 1.200 m.

Contrary to what Heuts and Leleup (1954) said that blind fish caves in this region are only located south of Mbanza-Ngungu, in this cave located north of Mbanza-Ngungu, blind fish were observed in 2006. However, today no specimen of this species is seen in this cave (Kimbembi, 2009). It is highly likely that this is the result of cannibalism by the *Clarias* that are in large numbers in this cave.

The Ngombe-Ntadi axis.

In this axis, a cave with blind fish has been identified: the Mbuzi cave. It is located to the southwest, between hamlets 2 and 3 of Ngombe-Ntadi at an altitude of 502 m.

9° Grotte de Mbuzi (n⁰ 21), 5° 18' 34.6" south latitude;14° 48' 34.7" south longitude

The Mbuzi cave is located 100 m to the south, in the extension of the Nkueke cave. Its entrance, facing west, forms a funnel 3 m deep. However, the cave itself has a south-east orientation. It is fed by three resurgences that form an underground watercourse with blind fish. Over a distance of 1 km, its depth, shallow at the beginning (20 cm), increases as one moves inside the cave until it reaches 2 m in depth. The Mbuzi cave is a new locality for blind fish discovered by Kimbembi (2009).

The Ebeya axis.

This axis includes a single cave.

10° Grotte d'Ebeya (n° 24), 5° 16' 32.7" south latitude; 14° 52' 54.6" east longitude

The Ebeya cave, formerly called the small cave of the military camp, is a cave that is located at 638 m above sea level, south of the Ebeya military camp. From the entrance, it includes an underground pool, with blind fish more or less large. This cave, which served as a water collection point for the water supply of the Ebeya military camp, is now abandoned. The southern direction of a small stream that flows out of it suggests the probable existence of a connection from this cave to the Ngovo cave.

The probable existence of a connection network between the different caves in this sector remains to be demonstrated. In-depth investigations, in the long term, are indispensable. Indeed, how can we explain the presence of *Caecobarbus geertsii* in the Ngovo and Ebeya caves, when it was not reported by Heuts and Leleup (1954).

IV.1.2 Caves in the South Gombe area

The caves explored by Heuts and Leleup (1954) were grouped into three sectors (I, II, III). And, according to these authors, *Caecobarbus geertsii* would only be found in the caves of sector I, i.e. in the surroundings of Mbanza-Ngungu, whose administrative sector is Boko.

However, the 2016-2017 *Caecobarbus* expeditions conducted in Area II revealed the presence of two caves (Muisi Cave in Kitala-Mpanga and Mambuela Cave in Kongo dia Kati) with blind fish. This shows that it is still important to recheck previous observations regarding the presence of *Caecobarbus* in the caves of Area II.

11° Muisi cave, it is located at 641 m of altitude at 05°49'44,3" of south latitude; 14°55'57,3" of east longitude.

The entrance to the cave that gives the opening to the west of the village (Fig. 18) appears to be a dry river in the dry season; it seems to function as an overflow to the river that lies further inside the cave. The entrance to the cave is about 3 meters wide. The height of the cave decreases the further inward you go, forcing visitors to crouch down. But it increases before reaching a perennial underground river, perpendicular to the entrance corridor. During the period of our investigations (dry season), this river persists in the form of pools that communicate with each other. It is in these pools of the river that *Caecobarbus* were observed (Fig. 19).

Fig. 18: Entrance to the Muisi cave

Fig. 19: *Caecobarbus geertsii* in one of the pools of the Muisi cave

12° Grotte de Mambuela (Grotte L. Van de Berghe; B26), 5°44'32.5"S latitude; 14°54'17.2"E longitude.

It is located southwest of the village of Kongo dia Kati at an altitude of 618 m. The cave is already known since the Belgian colonial period, discovered by Europeans in 1949 (Heuts and Leleup, 1954). This cave has two parts. In its right part, the big metallic ladder installed by the Belgians, allows the descent in the big chamber characterized by an impressive stalactite and "draperies".

Fig. 20 : Mambuela cave : stalactites with drapery aspect

In this part of the cave, dry in the dry season, no *Caecobarbus* was observed during our visit. To the left of this large chamber, a hole about 4 m deep, difficult to access without adequate equipment, receives the water coming from the left part of the same cave. However, in the left part of this cave, a slightly elevated cavity keeps permanent water (drinking water for the market gardeners). It is in this subterranean river with easy access in the first five meters that specimens of *Caecobarbus* were observed. Beyond five meters, the water touches the ceiling of the cave and does not allow access without more specialized equipment.

CHAPTER V: OUTLINE OF A STRUCTURE FOR THE MBANZA-NGUNGU CAVE BIOSPHERE RESERVE.

Taking into account the geographical, ecological and existential contexts of *Caecobarbus geertsii*, the general objective of our work is the proposal of the recognition of this cave area as a biosphere reserve with a cluster biosphere reserve configuration.

It will be about:

1. to set up the necessary management structures;
2. To obtain from national institutions the strengthening of the legislation for the protection and conservation of caves;
3. raise awareness and involve local communities
4. seek international expertise (UNESCO) on the project.

Management measures for the biosphere reserve must be taken on the basis of data obtained in the field. These measures must be specific to the characteristics of the sites considered.

Within the framework of the conservation of the caves identified in Zone I, nine core areas have been proposed. These are:

- central area I: Ebeya cave ;
- central area II: Lukatu cave;
- central area III: Ngovo cave;
- central area IV: Mankondo and Nzonzi caves;
- central area V: Kiamvu cave;
- central area VI: Nziulu caves;
- central area VII: Nkiengie cave complex;
- central area VIII: Kambu cave;
- central area IX: Mbuzi cave.

-    .l Territorial arrangement of the biosphere reserve (lïg. 21)

In practical terms, a biosphere reserve should include four distinct categories of areas (Maldague, 2003), namely:

- a central area ;

- a buffer zone;

- a transition area;

- associated areas.

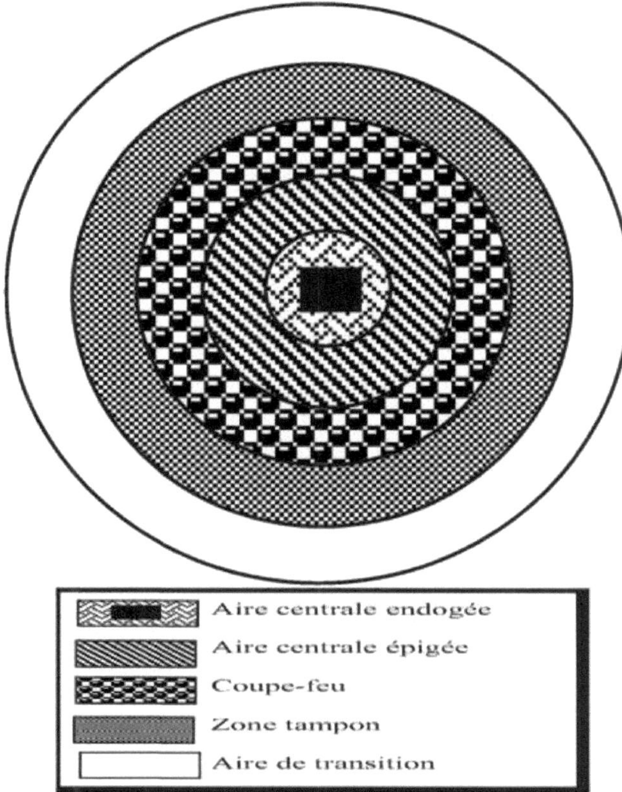

Fig. 21: Diagram of a minimum biosphere reserve

In the context of the Mbanza-Ngungu caves, the biosphere reserve must adopt the configuration of a cluster biosphere reserve. This expression refers to a group of non-contiguous areas that fulfill one or more of the biosphere reserve's functions.

Core Area Categories

For the protection of our caves, we envision two categories of core areas:

- the central endogenous area which corresponds to the cavity of the cave itself;
- the central epigean area which is on the surface of the ground and starts at the entrance of each cave and extends for 1 to 3 km outside the cave.

In other words, the core area of each cave consists of two parts: an endogenous core area, the cave *sensu stricto*, and an epigean core area.

- **Central endogenous area**

Types of endogenous central areas

Two types of core areas are considered depending on the degree of protection required:

- the central area, endogenous, with integral protection, where no visit of a tourist or economic nature is allowed;
- the mixed endogenous area, with integral protection, but where strictly controlled exceptions can be made in special cases.

- **Epigenetic central area**

Each endogenous core area will be surrounded by an epigenetic core area (1 to 3 km radius). This area must be well delineated. It will have full or mixed protection status, as will each of the endogenous core areas, and will be the open-air complement to them.

The function of the epigeous core areas is to protect the endogenous core area against any disturbance from outside. Different monitoring actions must be carried out there.

Both core and buffer areas will be permanently delineated, marked and identified by signs.

These areas must be legitimized, not only by ritualization, but also by the establishment of rights in order to make them inalienable by the different clans that participate in this delimitation.

- **Firestop**

A firebreak with a 100 m radius will be constructed between the spigot and the buffer zone. This firebreak must be impassable by fires coming from outside and must be regularly maintained.

- **Buffer zone**

Beyond the firewall, the core area is surrounded by a buffer zone that forms a 1 km radius ring. The buffer zone serves to isolate the core area from outside influences. In the buffer zone, only activities that are compatible with the purpose of the reserve (education and monitoring) are permitted.

- **Transition area**

The transition area, which is not strictly delineated, follows the buffer zone. It is in this area that actual recreational activities can be carried out.

- **Associated area or rehabilitation area**

As our knowledge of the caves in the area increases, it may be appropriate to include in the territorial layout plan one or more associated areas whose purpose or function would be to

rehabilitation of degraded caves. The associated area would receive in this case, the status of rehabilitation area.

V.2 Development principles

A certain number of development principles below must be strictly respected so that the fundamental characteristics and integrity of the Mbanza-Ngungu caves are safeguarded in the long term. **1° Delimitation of the area to be protected**

The use of concrete bollards or perennial stakes is recommended. Boundary markers should not be confusing in order to avoid land disputes between the area managers and the local population.

This work should include the strict delineation of not only the core area of the spigot, but also the buffer zone with firebreak demarcation.

2° Prohibition of all activities in the central areas

Once the delimitation and demarcation have been completed, all economic activities (agriculture, guano harvesting, etc.) and land use should be prohibited in the core areas (endogeous and epigeous). No road should cross the epigeous core areas.

3° Rehabilitation works (central endogenous area)

The endogenous core areas (caves themselves) should be rehabilitated as much as possible. These will consist of removing all that clutters them (foreign bodies), such as: debris and waste that not only affect the natural beauty of the caves, but also can harm their characteristics.

Such remediation operations have been undertaken in Ngovo Cave. They were executed with the greatest care, without harming the cave biodiversity.

4° Development work (central endogenous area)

In the Ngovo cave, the work consisted of the construction of concrete steps and the installation of metal ladders in the gallery at places with a steep slope.

5° Recreational and tourist facilities (endogenous central area)

The Ngovo cave can be occasionally opened for recreational activities. It falls into the category of a mixed endogenous core area. The management plan will specify the modalities of this use.

In terms of development, there are two categories: light development and heavy development.

6° Soil defense and restoration work (central area)

The epigenetic core area has a protective function for the endogenetic core area. Managers should establish an ongoing soil defense and restoration (SDR) program in this area. This work should include soil erosion control and maintenance of vegetative cover to mitigate the effects of rainfall (landslides, sheet erosion, etc.). This work shall include the firebreak area.

7° Access corridor (in the central area)

For the light development that will be required in the buffer zone and the epigenetic core area to allow visitor access, a minimum of infrastructure is required. An access track (or path) should be clearly marked and visitors should not be allowed to stray from it, in order to avoid environmental degradation.

Signage is essential. This one-way access trail will take visitors from the visitor center, located in the transition area at the entrance to the cave. This corridor must be marked.

8° Reception infrastructures

The visitor center falls into the category of heavy infrastructure. These do not belong in the core area or the buffer zone, so it is appropriate that the visitor center be located in the transition area.

The Visitor Center has an important educational and training role to play. To this end, it could include a museum section so that visitors can learn about the caves and their biodiversity before they even begin their visit. The visitor center may include a community shelter, straw huts, picnic areas and camping sites.

Such a center can be built near the Ngovo cave. The participation of the local population is essential to offer lucrative occupations.

V.3 Different functions of a biosphere reserve and management implications

1° *In situ* protection function

In the case of the Mbanza-Ngungu cave complex, this function is essentially aimed at protecting cave biodiversity and in particular that of *Caecobarbus geertsii*, which is totally dependent on these environments.

This function has implications for the management of these caves such as:

- integral protection of the endogenous core area;
- principle of prohibition of visits ;
- admission of a few annual visits to the mixed caves ;
- Prohibition of removal of biotic and abiotic material.

2° Research and monitoring function

This function is important, but it must be strictly controlled and not lead to negative impacts.

This function inspires caution which consists of:

- requirement of a legalized written research authorization ;
- restriction of the search operations to be performed ;

- qualitative and quantitative limitation of authorized withdrawals;
- obligation for any researcher to provide the results of his or her investigations.

3° Educational function

Visiting the protected area can help visitors understand the natural phenomena, make them understand their beauty and interest, and lead to greater respect for them. The activities are essentially observation. Photography by visitors is permitted.

The implications of this function are to:
- follow presentations before the site visit;
- to popularize cave information in written form;
- comply with the general provisions in force for visits;
- to familiarize the visitors with the cave environment.

4° Tourist and recreational function

Public awareness of environmental issues can be the basis for respecting the caves and their biodiversity. This tourist and recreational activity concerns especially the Ngovo cave.

This tourist function has the following implications
- organization of group relaxation moments ;
- awakening the spirit of observation and cultivating a love for nature;
- culture 1 of compliance with the instructions (consumption of food, drink, smoking and lighting any fire including torches).

Conclusion

In our work, it was a question of demonstrating that the caves of Mbanza-Ngungu in D.R. Congo, with the presence of *Caecobarbus geertsii, an* endemic and vulnerable fish species, constitute a potentiality of a world heritage property. However, this heritage that deserves conservation is currently in degradation.

Indeed, more than half a century later, the inventory of cave biodiversity in Sector I caves established by Kimbembi (2007), revealed not only the disappearance of two caves (cave B_{20} and cave B_{21}), out of the eight inventoried by Heuts and Leleup (1954), but also the disappearance of the blind fish population in three caves (Ebeya cave, Kambu cave and recently in the Lukatu cave)

Of all these blind fish caves inventoried by Heuts and Leleup (*op.cit.*), only two caves (Kiamvu Cave and Nkiengie Cave) still hold specimens of this species of fish. For the other three: the Nenga cave has not been revealed by the local population; the waterfall cave and the gas cave require adequate equipment for access. Thus, their real situation is unknown.

Fortunately, in this sector I, to the two old *Caecobarbus* stations that remained, eight new blind fish sites were added (Kimbembi, 2009). This gives a total of ten *Caecobarbus* ecosystems in this sector.

Having had an idea of the state of the cavernicolous biodiversity of sector I, in the framework of the continuous monitoring of these zones close to the threshold of irreversibility, our attention was focused today on the caves of sector II, with the aim of establishing also the state of the cavernicolous biodiversity of this zone. In fact, Heuts and Leleup (1954) did not report the presence of *Caecobarbus* in this sector.

While our expeditions to *Caecobarbus* (2016-2017) revealed the presence of two new caves to *Caecobarbus* in this sector including: the cave of Mambuela in Kongo dia Kati and the cave of Muisi in Kitala-Mpanga.

In short, in D.R. Congo, there are currently ten blind fish caves, ten of which are in sector I and two in sector II.

If measures to curb the degradation of these cryptic environments are not taken, the decline in blind fish localities may spread, especially in Sector I. While this fish species is listed in the IUCN red list as a vulnerable threatened species (Lévêque and Daget, 1984).

BIBLIOGRAPHY

BENSALEM, S., 1999. *Aspects relatifs à la législation, conventions internationales, politique de décentralisation*, ERAIFT- Unikin, RDC,31p.

BLACHE, J., 1967. *Les poissons du Tchad et du bassin adjacent du Mayo Kebbi, étude systématique et biologique* O.R.S.T.O.M., Paris, 483 P.

BOULENGER, G.A., 1921, Description d'un poisson aveugle découvert par M.G. Geerts dans la grotte de Thysville (Bas-Congo), *Rev. Zoologiques africaines* IX, F 3, pp. 232-233.

BRUEIL, H., 1952. The incised and punctuated figures of the Kiatapo caves, Katanga, *annals of the museum of the Belgian Congo*, 1,3 - 34.

CELINE, L., 2000. In the depths with the great white, *National Geographic mag.* 24, (7), pp. 54-75.

DE BROYER, C., 2005a. *Underground Biodiversity*, www. CWEPSS. ORG., 1 .

....

DE BOYER, C., 2005b. *The karst ecosystem, the roles of underground animals*, www. CWE PSS. ORG 1 p.

DE MARET, P., 1986. The Ngovo group: an industry with polished stone tools and pottery in lower Zaire, *African archaeological Review*, 4 (1986), 103-133.

DE MUNCK, J. and RAYMARKERS, P., 1961. Drawings and engravings in the Lovo complex, *Ngonge Kongo*, 10, R.D.C., p. 33.

EIGENMANN, C., 1909. Cave vertebrates of America, a study in degenerative evolution , *Carnegie inst. wash.publ.* N^0 104, 241 p.

GERARD, P., 1936. Sur l'existence de vestiges oculaires chez *Caecobarbus geertsii Memoir of the Royal Museum of Belgian History*, Brussels S2. Fasc.3,pp. 549-552.

GILLAIN, J., 1953. *Organisation and exploitation of livestock in the Belgian Congo, Volume 1, general zootechnics*, Brussels, 273 p.

GINET, R. and DECOU, V., 1977. *Initiation à la biologie et écologie souterraine*, Coll. universitaire, éd. Decarpe, Paris, 345 p.

HEUTS, M.J., 1951. Ecology, variation and adaptation of the blind African cave fish *Caecobarus geertsii* Blgr, *Annals Soc. Roy. Belgium.* 82 (2) 155-227.

HEUTS, M.J. and LELEUP, N., 1954. The geography and ecology of the Bas-Congo caves, the habitats of *Caecobarbus geertsii* Blg. *Ann. Mus. Roy. du Congo Belge, series in 8, J.C. Zool*, 35,71p.

HUBBS, C.L., 1938. Fishes from the caves of Yucatan Museum of zoology, university of Michigan, *Carnegie; Inst wash. Public*, 491: 261295.

HUTCHEON, 1995. *Natural resources exploited around Ankarana, cave fauna exploited in Ankarana, case of vertebrates*, Madagascar, 2 p.

JEANNEL, R., 1926. *Fauna cavernicole de la France avec une étude des conditions d'existence dans le domaine souterrain*, Encyclop. In tome 7, Paris, 334 p.

KABALA, M., 1976. *Aspect de la conservation de la nature au Zaïre*, ed. Lokole, Kinshasa, 312 p.

KIMBEMBI, M.I., 2007. *Approche systémique de la conservation des grottes de Mbanza-Ngungu, contribution à l'étude de la biodiversité cavernicole et proposition de création d'une aire protégée*, Ph.D. thesis, unpublished, ERAIFT, UNIKIN, R.D.Congo, 322 p.

KIMBEMBI, M.I., 2009. Discovery of new sites of *Caecobarbus geertsii* Blgr, 1921 in Mbanza-Ngungu, *Scientia* XVI (2009) 2 :227-239.

KIMBEMBI, M.I., 2012. Degradation of blind fish caves (*Caecobarbus geertsii* Boulenger, 1921, Teleostei Cyprinidae) in the Mbanza-Ngungu region of D.R.Congo and proposal for a protected area, *ANSD Bulletin*, vol. 13, September 2012, pp. 3138.

LELEUP, N., 1956. La faune cavernicole du Congo Belge et considérations sur les Coléoptères reliques d'Afrique intertropicale, *Annales du Musée Royal du Congo Belge, série in 8°, Sciences zoologiques, vol. 46*, Tervuren, 171 p.

LEVEQUE, C. and DAGET, J., 1984. *Check-list of the freshwater fishes of Africa (CLOFFA)*. In: DAGET, J., GOSSE, J.P. and THYS VAN AUDENAERDE, D., ORSTOM, Paris and MRAC, Tervuren, vol.1,pp. 217-342.

LEYSBETH, A., 1958. *The caves, their mysteries and their origins*, Bibliothèque de l'Etoile, Leverville, Belgian Congo, 48 p.

MALDAGUE, M., 2003, *Traité de gestion de l'environnement tropical, tome II, précis d'aménagement intégré du territoire, Analyse systémique appliquée à l'aménagement et à la gestion intégrés du territoire et des établissements humains (Treatise on the management of the tropical environment)*, UNESCO-MAB, Paris, 683 p.

MALDAGUE, M., MANKOTO, S. and RAKOTOMAVO, T., 1997. *Notions d'aménagement et de développement intégrés des forêts tropicales,* UNESCO, Paris, 378 p.

MANDJUMA, M., 1984. *Inventaire des grottes à dessins du Bas- Zaïre*, Musées Universitaires de Kinshasa, 17 p.

MINISTRY OF THE ENVIRONMENT CONSERVATION OF NATURE FISHERIES AND FORESTRY, 1998. *Arrêté n° 030/CA/MIN/ECNPF/98, du juillet 1998 portant réglementation du commerce international des espèces de la faune et flore sauvages menacées R.D.C.*, Kinshasa, 5 p.

MORTELMANS, G. and MONTEYNE, M.R., 1962. La grotte peinte de "Mbafu, témoignage iconographique de la 1ere évangélisation du Bas-Congo" *in* Actes du IVe congres panafricain de préhistoire et d'étude du quaternaire, Léopoldville, *Annales du M.R.A.C., série in 8 vol. 2 n° 40,* Tervuren, pp. 457-486.

MUTAMBUE, S., 1999. *Gestion rationnelle de la faune terrestre et aquatique, Chair 9*, ERAIFT-Unikin, Kinshasa, 1999, 9 p.

NELSON, J.S., 1994. *Fishes of the world*, 3rd ed. John Wiley & Sons, New York, 600 p.

OLIVEREAU, M. and HERLANT, M., 1954. Histological study of the hypophysis of *Caecobarbus geertsii* Blgr. *Bul.l de la classe des sciences*, 5ᵉ série, Bruxelles, Tome XL, pp. 50-51.

PELLEGRIN, J., 1926. Les poissons cavernicoles aveugles, *Révues générales des sciences pures et appliquées*, tome XXXVII, Paris, pp. 641643.

PELLEGRIN, J., 1930. Les Cyprinidés cavernicoles d'Afrique, *Archiv. Zool. Ital.* XVI, pp. 622-629.

PETIT, G., 1938. Au sujet du *Caecobarbus geertsii* Boulenger, extracted from the *Bulletin de la société zoologique* de France, Tome LXII, pp. 135141.

PETIT, G. and BESNARD, W., 1937. On the aquarium behavior of *Caecobarbus geertsii* Blgr, *Bull. Mus. Hist. Nat.2ᵉ ser.*, tome IX, Paris, 50-53.

Poll, M., 1953. The aquarium fishes of the Belgian Congo, *Bull.Soc. Royale Zool.* Antwerp, n⁰ 2, 48 p.

QUINIF, Y., 1985. *Kwilu-84, Expedition spéléologique dans le Bas-Zaïre*, Equipe spéléo du center, no 146, March 1985, Brussels, 9 p.

RAYMAKERS, P. and VAN MOORSEL, H., 1964. *Rock drawings of Bas-Congo-Lovo*. Ed. of the University of Leopoldville, 11p.

ROBERTS, R. T., 1975. Geographical distribution of African freshwater fishes, *Zool. J. Linn.* 57: 249-319, with 17 figures.

TEUGELS. G.G. and GUEGAN, J.F., 1994. Biological diversity of freshwater fishes of Lower Guinea and Central Africa, *Ann. Mus. Roy. Afr.Cent. Zool*, 275 : 67-85.

THINES, G., 1952. Recherches expérimentales sur la photosensibilité du poisson aveugle *Caecobarbus geertsii* Blgr, *Annales de la Soc Royale. Zool*, Belgium, 84: 231-265.

TUINES, G.and LEGRAIN, J.M., 1973. Effects of alarm substance on the behavior of cave fishes *Anoptichthys jordani* (Characidae) and *Caecobarbus geertsii* (Cyprinidae), *Ann. Spéleo.* 28, 2, pp. 291-297.

IUCN, 2001. *IUCN Red List Categories and Criteria: Version 3.1. IUCN Species Survival Commission,* Gland, Switzerland and Cambridge, UK, ii, 32 pp.

UNESCO, 1972. *Convention concerning the protection of the world cultural heritage adopted by the General Conference at its seventeenth session,* UNESCO, Paris, pp.23-33.

UNESCO, 1972. *Les biens inscrits sur la liste du patrimoine mondial, convention concernant la protection du patrimoine mondial, culturel et naturel,* Paris, 19 p.

VERVOORT, A., 1980. Karyotype of *Caecobarbus geertsii* Boulenger, (Teleostei: Cyprinidae), *the nuleus*, Rabat, vol.23 (1,2): 76-77.

www.betharram.com/, 2005. *Caves of Betharram, tourism in Lourdes-Pyrenees.*

www.culture.fr/arcnat/lascaux/lr/, 2004. *The cave of Lascaux.*

www.grotte.ch/, 2004. *Tourist cave of Switzerland.*

www.grottes-medous.com/, 2005. *Caves of Medous, stalactites, concretions, stalagmites*.

Printed by Books on Demand GmbH, Norderstedt / Germany